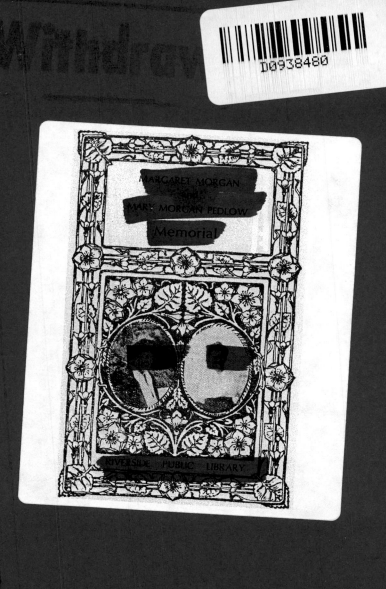

Spiritual Biographies
FOR YOUNG READERS

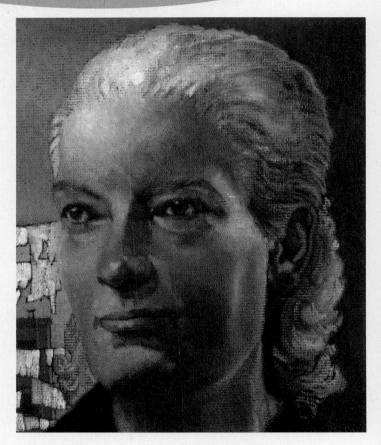

Dorothy Day
A Catholic Life of Action

Maura D. Shaw • Illustrations by Stephen Marchesi

Walking Together, Finding the Way
SKYLIGHT PATHS Publishing
Woodstock, Vermont

Who Was Dorothy Day?

Dorothy Day began her lifelong work of helping hungry and homeless people when she was a young newspaper reporter in New York City. In 1933, during the Great Depression, she and her friend Peter Maurin started a newspaper called the *Catholic Worker* so they could tell the world that people needed food for the body and also food for the soul. Dorothy lived out her beliefs in very practical ways; she didn't just talk about what good things should be done—she did them. She set up houses and farms where people in need could find work, food, friends, and community. She worked in soup kitchens, and she prayed every day. She tried to "see" God in the face of each person she met.

When you learn about Dorothy Day's life, you will see what makes her amazing. Through the Catholic Worker movement and the way that she lived her life, Dorothy taught people that we show our love for God by loving and helping our fellow human beings.

Dorothy hard at work at her typewriter.

Dorothy's Good Work

Dorothy Day believed that we all can do good work in the world by helping other people.

"We begin with ourselves and give what we have, and the movement spreads," she said.

She understood about sharing and giving because she lived a long time on the Lower East Side of New York City, where people were poor but were known for their hospitality. Dorothy remembered someone saying, "There is always enough for one more. Everyone just takes a little less."

Standing Up for Her Beliefs

Dorothy Day grew up in a family where money was hard to come by. Often the children ate only bread and jelly and bananas for supper. As a young woman, Dorothy became a reporter and wrote stories about the poor people she met in New York. Besides trying to convince rich people to share their wealth with those who had nothing, Dorothy also protested against the war raging around the world. Dorothy was a pacifist, a believer in peace and solving conflicts without violence; she never changed her opinion about this over the rest of her long life.

When she was only twenty, in 1917, Dorothy went to jail for the first time—not for committing a crime, but for marching outside the White House with other women demanding the right to vote. Like Mahatma Gandhi and Martin Luther King Jr., Dorothy Day was not afraid to stand up for her beliefs.

Dorothy, *left,* at an antiwar protest in 1916, before America entered World War I.

While Dorothy was in jail, she began to read the Bible.

The suffering and poverty in the neigh-borhoods where she lived touched Dorothy's heart deeply. It didn't seem that much was being done to help people. She soon came to see that Roman Catholic churches were one place where the poor, especially immigrants, were welcomed and cared for with God's love.

An old postcard showing
Our Lady of Help of Christians Church,
where Dorothy was baptized.

From her curiosity about what she called the "church of the poor," Dorothy Day slowly came to believe that every one of us is asked to become God's mercy in our daily actions. We are asked to feed, clothe, shelter, and love one another—providing for one another as God provides for us. After her only child, a daughter she named Tamar, was born, Dorothy was baptized into the Catholic Church. Her life's work was only just beginning.

The Beginning of the *Catholic Worker*

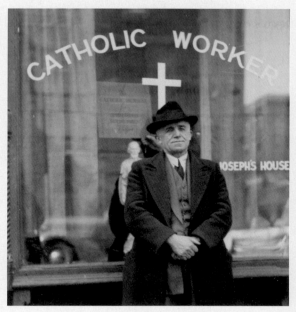

Peter Maurin, cofounder of the *Catholic Worker*.

Dorothy Day went to a march against hunger in Washington, D.C., in 1932 to remind the government that people were suffering in the Great Depression. Sad and angry, she prayed hard for a chance to use her talents to help. When she returned to New York, a French man named Peter Maurin was waiting to meet her. He was just as eager as Dorothy was to fight poverty, hunger, and other social problems in the spirit of the teachings of Jesus. Together they decided to publish a monthly newspaper called the *Catholic Worker*. They raised money and found volunteers to write and illustrate the newspaper. The first issue was sold on the streets in 1933, for a penny a copy. Many were given away free.

Dorothy and Peter both wrote articles for the *Catholic Worker* about the need to help people, and soon they put their beliefs into practice. They began to set up "houses of hospitality" for men and women in New York's poorest areas. Volunteers helped run the houses and make soup for all the hungry people.

The work at the hospitality houses was never-ending, and often the volunteers and the guests quarreled and complained. Dorothy sometimes lost her temper, though she tried not to. But she found strength in prayer, in attending daily Mass, and in reading the Psalms. She believed it was just as important to feed the soul as to feed the body.

Dorothy Day, *far right,* and other volunteers at the *Catholic Worker.*

Creating Communities

From the first house on Fifteenth Street in New York City, the Catholic Worker movement spread to other houses, to other cities, and even to country farms. Dorothy Day wanted to create communities where people could earn their living, growing fruit and vegetables and raising livestock. Many of the guests at the farms were city people who didn't have the skills for farming, which made life a challenge. Later some of the farms became retreat centers where many people gathered for prayer, study, and peace.

Dorothy reading to Tamar.

Dorothy's daughter loved the farm life. She understood, as Dorothy did, that God can be found in nature. Tamar liked to spin thread and weave cloth, and later she grew her own flax to make linen thread. Dorothy said this gave Tamar "a feeling and a knowledge of ... God's creation.... And to plant a bed of flax is to see a most heavenly blue mass of flowers."

Dorothy, *second from right,* visits the Milwaukee Catholic Worker
Community's Holy Family House.

Dorothy's Hard Workers

Many young people were drawn to the Catholic Worker movement, to the great delight of Dorothy Day—if they were hard workers, that is. She had no patience for people who just sat around and talked while there were potatoes to peel or dishes to wash. And most of the young volunteers lived up to her hopes for them.

"When young people come here," she said, "we are grateful for their interest. I have watched some of them, trying so hard to talk with those men and women standing in line or sitting with their coffee and soup. The students know so much, and yet they are learning. The poor who come here feel there is little they have to offer anyone, and yet they have a lot to offer. The giving and the receiving is not only going on in one direction."

Now It's Your Turn

PUBLISH YOUR OWN NEWSPAPER

 Back in the 1930s, Dorothy Day believed that a newspaper was the best way to get important messages to people. The Catholic Worker newspaper is still published today—and it still sells for one penny a copy. What do you think is important to tell people? Do you have some good news to share? Or do you want to tell people how they can help make the world a better place? How would your information help them?

You can publish your own newspaper in many different ways. You can make a fancy one on a computer, at home or at school or at the library, and print out copies. Or you can write one by hand and make photocopies for your friends. You can create just one copy and pass it around.

You and your friends can be the reporters and write about what you want people to know. You each can draw your own pictures to illustrate the newspaper stories. You can even have a comics section, if you like. A funny cartoon is a wonderful way to get a message across.

THE CATHOLIC WORKER

October

Subscription: 25¢ Per Year

Price 1

Waiters

TEMPLE

come a metaphor.
More objections come from less literary cerns; for instance, that I avoid the spiritual Why do I not consider those waits as occa-...s to practice contemplation at last? Apart from (or as part of) my temperament, I have to say that much of what I have read...nds too abstract, far removed fro...'s real- ity. Not all, of cours...
Evelyn Underhil... where sh... this...

...ic on ...one line finally fil- me from Deane Mowrer who and blind. (She lived at the nid-50s, when her affliction set of cancer at Maryhouse in ays cited it to refer to the con- pen to her as her active life having a contemplative anaged to do was terpretation rent

O, INSTEAD
WHAT YOU
LOVE
AND LOVE G
AND, INSTEAD OF Y
YOU THINK ARE
HATE THE APPETIT
IN YOUR
WHICH ARE THE C
IF YOU LOVE PEACE, T
HATE TYRANN
BUT HATE THESE THING
NOT IN ANOTHER.
~~THOMAS MERTON

EACE,

PEOPLE
ERS,
SORDER

AR.
NJUSTICE
REED~
RSELF,

15

Calligraphy by Sabra McKenzie-Hamil

Spreading the Catholic Worker Message

Dorothy Day and Peter Maurin spread their ideas as far and as wide as the *Catholic Worker* newspaper could be sent. Dorothy often traveled to talk about their work—to anyone who would listen, anywhere. People donated money and property to be used for the hospitality houses, and others gave their time and energy.

The Catholic Worker movement asked people to freely choose

Dorothy was inspired by the life of Jesus, shown here caring for the sick.

to live in poverty so that the needs of others could be filled, to feed the hungry, to shelter the homeless, to resist war in every time and place, and to live in community with others. These ideas were based on the way that Catholic monks and nuns lived in the Middle Ages, when anyone in need could find food and shelter in a monastery. Today there are more than 150 Catholic Worker communities around the world.

Dorothy and a pair of young monks serving the needy.

Sharing Together

Dorothy Day showed respect for every person, rich or poor, easygoing or difficult. One day while the guests were eating lunch at a hospitality house, a tall, shaggy man came in and started shouting angrily. The people at the tables were afraid. Dorothy calmly invited the man to have a bowl of soup with her and brought two bowls to a table. The man did not eat but watched Dorothy take spoonfuls of her soup. Then he grabbed Dorothy's bowl and began to gobble her soup. He looked over at his own bowl and Dorothy asked, "Would you like *me* to eat *your* soup?"

Every day a long line of people waited for bread at the Mott Street Catholic Worker house in New York City during the Great Depression.

Dorothy realized the man didn't trust anyone and thought his soup might have had something bad put into it. He nodded, and Dorothy ate his soup. Then she shared her piece of bread with him. The man ate his half and left.

The next morning the tall man returned with a brown paper bag stuffed with carrots, potatoes, onions, and celery. "To make more soup," he said to Dorothy. And he became a regular guest at the house.

Dorothy Day's Lifelong Work

Dorothy grew older and her hair turned snow white. She continued to live and work in the hospitality houses, and she never lost her passion for writing and speaking about God's love for us. When asked about her long life, she said, "If I have accomplished anything in my life, it is because I wasn't embarrassed to talk about God."

During all the wars of the twentieth century, Dorothy Day kept firm to her pacifist beliefs, even when it made her—and the Catholic Worker movement—unpopular. She acted on her own beliefs and expected others to act on theirs.

Dorothy Day lived to be eighty-three years old. Many people said that

Dorothy reads with her grandchildren.

she was a saint—a very human kind of saint. The Catholic Church may someday declare her to be one, but how would Dorothy herself have felt about that? When a reporter once told her that it was the first time he had interviewed a saint, she replied, "Don't call me a saint—I don't want to be dismissed that easily." What she meant was that she didn't have any special strengths or abilities that helped her to do what she did—it was just plain hard work, prayer, and God's love, which is given to every single person on earth. We are all called by God to love one another as God loves us.

That's the message of Dorothy Day.

Fascinating Fact

Someone once told Dorothy Day that she was hot-headed and lost her temper too often. "I hold more temper in one minute than you will hold in your entire life," she replied.

KEEP OUT OF WAR

THE CATHOLIC WORKER

An Amazing Life

Dorothy Day began her real life's work when she saw that God was present within every person she met. Giving food to the hungry, giving shelter to the homeless, giving love to the people whom others pretend not to see, Dorothy Day created the worldwide Catholic Worker movement—one bowl of soup at a time. Isn't that amazing?

 # Inspired by Jesus' Blessings

Dorothy Day read the words of Jesus in the Bible and took them to heart. She lived her life in honor of the Beatitudes, or blessings, that she found in his teachings:

"How blessed are the poor in spirit; the kingdom of heaven is theirs." (Matthew 5:3)

"Blessed are the peacemakers; they shall be recognized as children of God." (Matthew 5:9)

"In truth I tell you, in so far as you did this to one of the least of these brothers of mine, you did it to me." (Matthew 25:40)

Now It's Your Turn
BUILD A MOUNTAIN

 The world still has many hungry people. Some of them live in your own town or city. Soup kitchens and food pantries, where people can get a free meal or food to take home for their families, are always in need of help.

If there is a hospitality house or community center near you, maybe you and your family could volunteer for a few hours. If you can help clear dishes from the table at home, you can help clear the bowls from the tables at the soup kitchen.

Another way to offer help is by collecting donations of food for homeless shelters and food pantries. Ask the principal of your school if you can make a mountain of cereal in the school lobby. Boxes of cereal are easy for kids to carry to school. Each classroom might want to build its own mountain. The colorful stacks are fun to look at, and if they topple over they won't hurt anyone. If you collect enough cereal boxes for a mountain, the hospitality house will be glad for the help. If you only collect a hill of boxes, they'll still be happy!

High school student Jeff Glick collected a mountain of cereal
to give to the food pantries in his town so that poor children
would have breakfast every day.

Now It's Your Turn
A LOVING HEART

 "The great need of the human heart is for love," said Dorothy Day.

On a piece of paper, draw a big heart with a crayon or pencil. Now fill in the heart with pictures or words about what matters to you.

What is in your heart? Who and what do you love? And why?

Important Events in the Life of Dorothy Day

1897—Dorothy Day was born in Brooklyn Heights, New York. She later moved with her family to California and Chicago.

1916—Dorothy went to New York City to work as a reporter, writing about the poor and about the peace movement during World War I.

1917—She spent thirty days in jail for marching to demand women's right to vote. In jail she began to read the Bible.

1920s—She visited Catholic churches in New York, at first because she was curious and later because she was impressed with how warmly the churches welcomed immigrants.

1927—Dorothy Day was baptized as a Roman Catholic, believing that she was joining "the church of the poor."

1933—She and Peter Maurin started a monthly newspaper, the *Catholic Worker*, which later expanded to become the foundation for a worldwide movement.

1933—Dorothy Day and Peter Maurin opened the first Catholic Worker "houses of hospitality" for people needing food and shelter during the Great Depression.

1936—The New York Catholic Worker community opened its first farm, in Easton, Pennsylvania, called Maryfarm.

1948—A collection of Dorothy's writing was published in a book called *On Pilgrimage*.

1952—*The Long Loneliness*, Dorothy's autobiography, was published.

1960s—Dorothy was busy traveling and speaking around the world. She protested against war and dedicated her life to peace.

1963—Dorothy published *Loaves and Fishes*, a book about the first thirty years of the Catholic Worker movement.

1977—On Dorothy's eightieth birthday, Cardinal Cooke, the archbishop of New York, visited her to deliver a personal greeting from Pope Paul VI.

1980—Dorothy Day died peacefully at the age of eighty-three.

2000—The Holy See at the Vatican in Rome opened a cause for the beatification and canonization of Dorothy Day. She may one day officially be named a "saint."

Important Words to Know

Great Depression The worldwide economic disaster that occurred in the 1930s. In the United States, one worker out of every four could not find a job.

Hospitality Offering the gift of food and shelter to another person.

Immigrant A person who leaves the country where he or she was born and starts a new life in another country.

Mass The main worship service of the Roman Catholic Church.

Monastery The house of a community of monks or nuns, where they live, pray, and work.

Pacifist Someone who believes only in the use of peaceful ways to solve problems and is opposed to war and the use of any violence.

Psalms One of the books of the Bible. People often read the Psalms for comfort and inspiration.

Saint A person whose life shows holiness and special closeness to God. As a Catholic, Dorothy Day officially would be declared a saint by the pope, who is the head of the Roman Catholic Church.

Volunteer Someone who freely offers to work or to help someone else, without payment.

Dorothy Day:
A Catholic Life of Action

2004 First Printing
Text and illustrations © 2004 by SkyLight Paths Publishing

Library of Congress Cataloging-in-Publication Data
Shaw, Maura D.
Dorothy Day : A Catholic Life of Action / Maura D. Shaw ; illustrations by Stephen Marchesi.
       p. cm. — (Spiritual biographies for young readers)
ISBN 1-59473-011-3 (hardcover)
1. Day, Dorothy, 1897–1980—Juvenile literature. 2. Catholics—United States—Biography—Juvenile literature. 3. Social reformers—United States—Biography—Juvenile literature. [1. Day, Dorothy, 1897–1980. 2. Reformers. 3. Women—Biography.] I. Marchesi, Stephen, ill. II. Title. III. Series.
BX4705.D283 S53 2004
267'.182'092—dc22

                                                   2003023614

Manufactured in China

10 9 8 7 6 5 4 3 2 1

A special thank you to Shelly Angers for her help in creating the activities in this book. Thank you also to Philip Runkel, archivist in the Department of Special Collections and University Archives at Marquette University Library in Milwaukee, Wisconsin, for his help with selecting photographs and his editorial suggestions.

The news photograph on page 27 by Bonnie G. Glick first appeared in the *Poughkeepsie Journal* and is used here with the kind permission of the copyright holder. No affiliation with or sponsorship by the manufacturers whose products are shown in the photograph is claimed or implied. Photograph © Bonnie G. Glick.

Grateful acknowledgment is given for permission to reprint photographs from the following sources: the Marquette University Archives, United Press International (p. 6), Henry Beck (p. 9), Michael Strasser (p. 12), the *Catholic Worker* newspaper (p. 15), and Mottke Weissman (p. 24). Illustrations on page 28 are included courtesy of Shelly Angers, Briana Otranto, Madison Simler, Bridgett Taylor, and Kristi Templeton. Some images © Clipart.com.

SkyLight Paths Publishing is creating a place where people of different spiritual traditions come together for challenge and inspiration, a place where we can help each other understand the mystery that lies at the heart of our existence.

SkyLight Paths sees both believers and seekers as a community that increasingly transcends traditional boundaries of religion and denomination—people wanting to learn from each other, walking together, finding the way.

SkyLight Paths, "Walking Together, Finding the Way" and colophon are trademarks of LongHill Partners, Inc., registered in the U.S. Patent and Trademark Office.

Walking Together, Finding the Way
Published by SkyLight Paths Publishing
A Division of LongHill Partners, Inc.
Sunset Farm Offices, Route 4, P.O. Box 237
Woodstock, VT 05091
Tel (802) 457-4000   Fax (802) 457-4004
www.skylightpaths.com